VACCINATED

THE HISTORY AND SCIENCE OF IMMUNISATION

BY SARAH RIDLEY

FRANKLIN WATTS

LONDON • SYDNEY

HAVE YOU BEEN VACCINATED?

When you were a baby, your parents or carers probably took you for your jabs, or vaccinations. These protect you against infectious diseases that used to kill millions of people around the world every year. Depending on where you live and your health, your doctor will decide which vaccines you need.

In many countries, babies are vaccinated against rotavirus (see page 4), a virus which causes a nasty stomach bug.

WHAT IS A VACCINE?

A vaccine is a medicine that is put into the body to prevent a harmful infectious disease, or diseases. It usually takes several years for scientists and doctors to work out how to make a vaccine. Despite years of trying, it hasn't been possible to develop vaccines against all serious diseases.

In April 2021, a group of scientists announced that they had developed a successful vaccine against malaria, a disease spread by the female Anopheles mosquito.

PREVENTION, NOT CURE

A vaccine prevents people from developing a particular disease rather than curing them. Since we only have vaccines against a few diseases, it is important to stay healthy by exercising, getting enough sleep, keeping clean and eating a good range of healthy foods.

FROM EPIDEMIC TO PANDEMIC

Sometimes a new disease emerges, often caused by a new virus. It spreads so fast that it becomes an epidemic, with large numbers of people falling ill in the same area. When the disease spreads to countries around the world, it becomes a pandemic. This happened in 2020 when the SARS-CoV-2 virus (see pages 26–27), and the Covid-19 disease it causes, spread around the world.

In spring 2020, governments around the world told people to stay at home and wash their hands regularly to help stop the spread of Covid-19. Here a firefighter sprays a playground in Malaysia with chemicals to kill the virus.

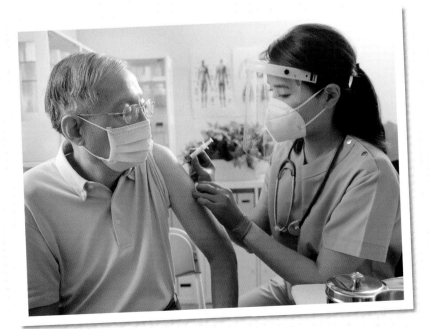

Since older people were at most risk of dying from Covid-19, they were some of the first to receive the vaccine.

VACCINES IN A HURRY

At first everyone felt helpless. While there were some medicines that helped patients, there was no cure for the disease. But soon scientists and doctors worked out which virus was causing the disease, and then serious vaccine research could begin. Due to the hard work and talent of scientists and doctors, people started receiving the first vaccinations against Covid-19 by the end of 2020.

GERMS AND THE IMMUNE SYSTEM

But let's go back to the start. What causes infectious diseases? Germs. These tiny living things are so small you need a microscope to see them. When germs, such as viruses, bacteria and fungi, get inside your body, they start to make more of themselves and this makes you feel ill. Luckily you have an immune system which springs into action against them.

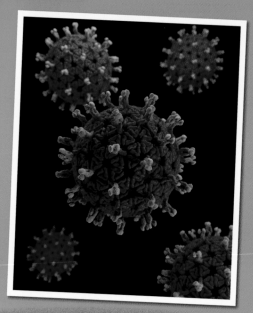

Like most viruses, rotaviruses are so small that they can only be seen by using a powerful electron microscope.

WHAT IS YOUR IMMUNE SYSTEM?

Your immune system includes your skin, salty tears, the lining of your nose, throat, lungs and stomach, the saliva in your mouth and special cells found in your blood and elsewhere. They work together to act as a barrier and catch, attack and kill invading germs, also called microbes. Most microbes are harmless. In fact, trillions of microbes live inside your body, helping it digest food and keeping you healthy.

Most of the time, your immune system prevents germs from getting inside your body. If germs do get inside, white blood cells can rush to the area, grab hold of them, pull them inside their cell walls and destroy them. At the same time, you might develop a high temperature, or fever, which is your immune system trying to slow down or kill the germs.

One way germs spread is when an infected person sneezes or coughs near others, who breathe in the germs.

This illustration shows a macrophage (right), a type of white blood cell, pulling a bacterium (left) into itself to 'digest' and destroy it. You'd need a powerful microscope to see this.

If this fails to destroy the germs, your body has a second line of defence. It is made up of two more types of white blood cell: T-cells and B-cells.

T-CELLS AND B-CELLS

Viruses multiply inside some of your cells, making them into virus factories. To stop this process, T-cells search out these infected cells and make them self-destruct. Meanwhile, B-cells work out exactly which markers, or antigens, lie on the surface of the germ. They start producing Y-shaped antibodies which are just the right shape to fit onto some of the antigens.

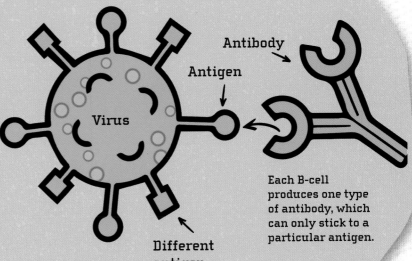

Antibody

Antigen

Virus

Different antigen

Each B-cell produces one type of antibody, which can only stick to a particular antigen.

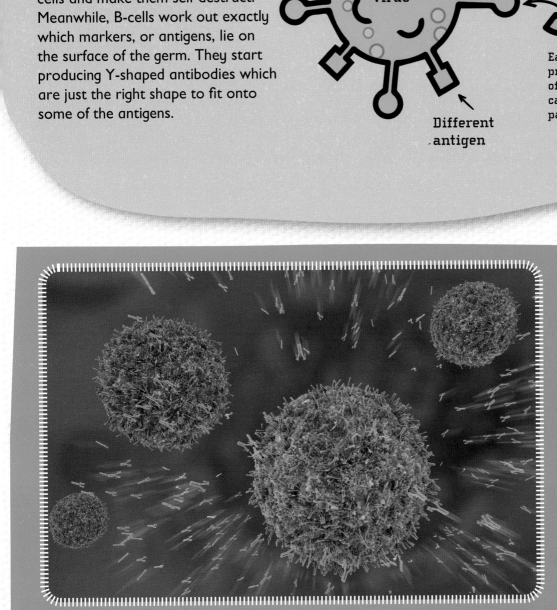

Y-shaped antibodies rush to attach themselves to the antigens on the outside of viruses. Once B-cells have worked out how to make the right antibody, they make masses of them.

When antibodies stick to the antigens on a germ, they slow it down, smother it or mark it out for destruction by other white blood cells. You start to feel better and recover. A few antibodies stay in your blood. Meanwhile, some B- and T-cells become memory cells, able to recognise this particular germ and be ready to fight it off if it comes back. You are now immune to that particular germ.

PREVENTING INFECTIONS

For a long time in human history, no one knew how or why people became ill. Were the stars in the wrong place or was a god unhappy? Did bad smells in the air carry illnesses? As far back as the ancient Greeks, it was noticed that people rarely had the same illness twice but, without microscopes to see germs, people didn't know how infections were spread.

This is the Hindu goddess Sitala. People in North India and Bengal worshipped Sitala from the 12th century onwards, hoping she could cure their smallpox. Some Hindus still pray to her if their children have measles or chicken pox.

SITALA.
GODDESS OF SMALLPOX.

VARIOLATION

One breakthrough in preventing infections started over 500 years ago in China. Medical practitioners started performing variolation to protect people against smallpox, a deadly disease that caused the skin to break out in spots. Scabs or pus were collected from someone with smallpox. The scabs could be ground up or soaked in water, and the pus was placed on a cotton swab. Whichever method was chosen, the resulting concoction was either blown up, or placed in, the nose.

Disgusting as it sounds, it worked because it introduced a tiny amount of the disease into the body, causing a mild case of smallpox. The person's immune system fought off the disease and developed antibodies to smallpox. Another way to do it was to scratch the skin and place smallpox scab powder or pus into the scratch. In parts of Asia and Africa, variolation protected many people from smallpox.

This illustration compares the development of cowpox and smallpox scabs. Scabs which looked like the one marked 20th (day) were used for variolation.

Cow Pox.   Small Pox.

8.th Day

10.th

12.th

18.th   20.th

12.th

EARLY UNDERSTANDING OF DISEASE

Around the world, groups of people discovered that eating certain plants helped the sick recover from illness, but they didn't know why. They also discovered that quarantines helped slow the spread of certain diseases. During the medieval period in Europe (roughly 11th to the 15th centuries), epidemics of plague and other infectious diseases often broke out. Towns used quarantine laws to prevent ships from coming into port for a month, or ordered infected people to stay inside their homes, but they still didn't know that germs spread diseases.

THE FIRST MICROSCOPE

Then in the 17th century, people began to unlock the secret world of microbes using new inventions. Dutchman Antonie van Leeuwenhoek (1632–1723) used the newly invented microscope, a single-lensed machine of his own design. To his amazement, he saw tiny things in a drop of water. What he thought were tiny animals were in fact bacteria. It was over a hundred years before Louis Pasteur (see page 18) proved that some of these bacteria spread diseases.

This print shows red crosses painted on London doors to mark which households were in quarantine during the Great Plague of the 1660s. They had to stay inside for 40 days.

Antonie van Leeuwenhoek was able to magnify objects by up to 200 times using his simple hand-held microscope. Other microscopes were invented soon afterwards.

SMALLPOX: FROM VARIOLATION TO VACCINE

Smallpox! This dreadful disease caused epidemics for thousands of years. It spread in the air when infected people coughed or sneezed, and by touch, when people came into contact with spots or infected bed linen. It killed about a third of the people who caught it, and survivors were often left with terrible scars or became blind. Slowly the knowledge that variolation (see page 6) could prevent smallpox spread from Asia and Africa to Europe and the USA.

LADY MARY

The person who brought variolation to Europe was Lady Mary Wortley Montagu (1689–1762). She heard about variolation when she was living in Constantinople, modern Istanbul, with her husband. Since smallpox had killed her brother and left her with scars, she was keen to protect her children. In 1718, she had her son variolated. A Turkish woman, a local expert, pricked the boy's arm with a needle loaded with the virus, while a British doctor rubbed smallpox pus into scratches on his other arm. Back home in Britain, she asked the same doctor to variolate her daughter in 1721. Word spread about this new way of preventing smallpox and Lady Mary encouraged others to seek protection.

Lady Mary wore thick make-up to cover up the scars left by smallpox.

NOT WITHOUT RISKS

Variolation, a method of inoculation, protected people from serious smallpox but it did cause a mild case of the disease. People needed to stay at home at this time as it was possible to spread smallpox to others. Sometimes, if variolation was not done correctly, the person became very ill with smallpox or even died.

COTTON MATHER

Meanwhile, a US churchman called Cotton Mather (1663–1728) encouraged people to get themselves inoculated during an epidemic of smallpox in Boston in the USA in 1721. His slave, Onesimus, had been inoculated as a child in Africa and told Mather how it was done. Mather tried to get doctors interested in the idea but only managed to persuade one doctor, Zabdiel Boylston (1679–1766), to start variolating people.

Cotton Mather is famous for introducing variolation to the USA. The method involved making scratches in the skin and rubbing smallpox pus into them.

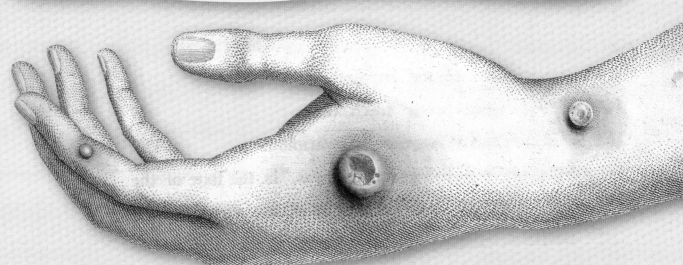

Cowpox caused sores on the hands, arms and face, and it also made people feel slightly ill for a few days.

MILKMAIDS AND COWPOX

Now the story moves to Gloucestershire, England. Here a country doctor called Edward Jenner (1749–1823) became intrigued by local stories that milkmaids, young women who milked cows for a living, had clear skin because they hardly ever caught smallpox. They did however catch cowpox from their cows. What was going on?

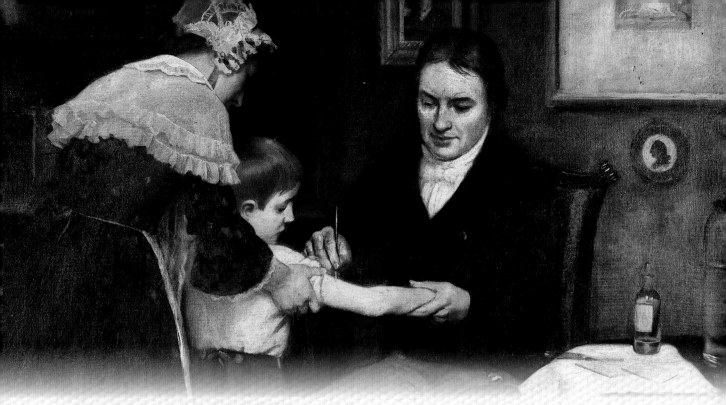

JENNER'S EXPERIMENT

Dr Jenner had been inoculated against smallpox as a child and used the technique to protect his own patients against smallpox, but was there a safer way to do this? Alongside his other work, he wondered: if I deliberately infect someone with cowpox, a less serious disease that seems to be similar to smallpox, will it protect them from deadly smallpox?

In 1796, when a milkmaid called Sarah Nelmes visited Dr Jenner to ask advice about her rash, he realised she had cowpox. He decided to test his idea. He collected some pus from her cowpox sores, scratched the arm of his gardener's eight-year-old-son, James Phipps, and rubbed some of the cowpox pus into the scratches.

James developed one spot soon afterwards and felt slightly ill. Six weeks later, Dr Jenner repeated the experiment but this time he rubbed smallpox pus into scratches on James' arm. Thankfully James did not develop smallpox. Dr Jenner had developed the first vaccine, protecting people against smallpox by stimulating their immune system to create antibodies against cowpox, a much milder disease.

In this painting Dr Edward Jenner is using a blade to scratch James Phipps' skin, before rubbing in cowpox pus on 14 May 1796. This was the first vaccination.

HESITANCY

Dr Jenner wrote about his experiment and its results, repeated the experiment on several other people including his own son, and published his research in a book. However, many people remained unsure about vaccinations for different reasons. These included:
- loss of income from variolating (inoculating) people
- finding it difficult to get hold of cowpox material for vaccinations
- not liking the fact that the vaccines had anything to do with cows
- not being able to see or understand why the vaccine worked.

Dr Jenner called his summerhouse the Temple of Vaccinia. He vaccinated people for free at a time when there was no free medical care.

THE TEMPLE OF VACCINIA

Despite vaccine hesitancy, Dr Jenner devoted himself to vaccinating people against smallpox and turned a summerhouse in his garden into the first vaccination centre! He also taught others how to vaccinate safely and supplied them with cowpox material for the vaccines.

In this portrait of Dr Jenner, the painter has shown cows. This reminds us that cowpox material in his vaccine protected people against smallpox.

Gradually vaccinations caught on around the world. Dr Jenner received gifts, medals and degrees to honour his work. He knew that his vaccine worked but he didn't know exactly why. It would be over a hundred years before scientists and doctors could see the smallpox virus, when the invention of the electron microscope allowed people to see viruses for the first time in the 1930s.

HOW DO VACCINES WORK?

A vaccine works by teaching your immune system how to recognise a harmful germ and learn how to fight it without having to go through the illness. If the germ gets inside your body at a future date, your immune system will recognise it, and more importantly, know how to destroy it so that you don't fall ill.

Vaccines are stored in bottles called vials until they are needed.

INFECTION VS. VACCINATION

In most cases, people who survive an infectious disease have more protection than someone who has been vaccinated against the same disease. Why? Because when your body fights off a disease it produces many different antibodies that work against different antigens on the surface of the germ. However, the hitch is that you might not survive, or you might be ill for a long time or parts of your body may be damaged by the illness.

DEVELOPING IMMUNITY

A vaccine is usually made from a weakened or dead version of the germ, tiny parts of a germ or instructions so that the body can make the germ's antigen. A few vaccines, including Dr Jenner's smallpox vaccine, use a weak version of a similar but less serious disease.

WHAT'S IN A VACCINE?

After a vaccination, your immune system attacks the harmless form of the germ in the vaccine in the same way as it attacks other invading germs (see pages 4–5).

1. There are already antibodies in your blood against different germs.

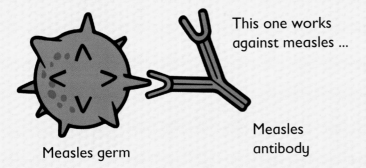

This one works against measles ...

Measles germ

Measles antibody

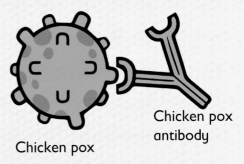

This one works against chicken pox.

Chicken pox antibody

Chicken pox

2. There is no antibody against the new germ.

New germ

3. Your white blood B-cells start to work out how to create antibodies that fit the antigens on the surface of the dead or deactivated germs, or the tiny parts of the germ, in the vaccine.

Deactivated germ

4. It may take a few days for your immune system to produce the right antibodies. Success! The new antibodies fit the germ's antigens like a key in a lock.

New antibody

5. While this is happening, your immune system makes memory cells. Now if you catch the disease, the memory cells will remember which antibodies to make to fight this particular germ. You are immune and do not fall ill, or only mildly so.

VACCINATION DELIVERY

Most vaccinations involve injections although a few can be sprayed up the nose or dropped into the mouth. That's because scientists know injections are the best way to get most vaccines into your body without them being destroyed by acids in your mouth and stomach. The invention of the hypodermic syringe in the 1850s made it much quicker and easier to vaccinate people.

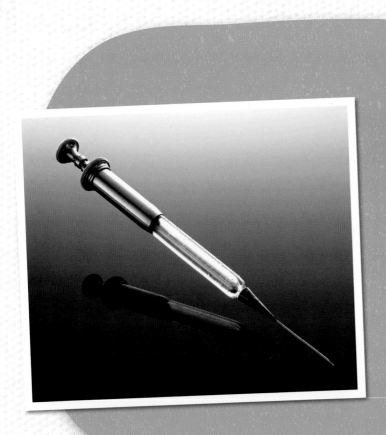

A hypodermic syringe, dating from 1855–65. It uses Alexander Wood's (1817–1854) invention where he joined a hypodermic needle to a glass body and added a plunger to deliver the vaccine into the body as an injection.

Benjamin Rubin (1917–2010) invented the bifurcated needle in the 1960s. It holds a dose of smallpox vaccine between its prongs, which pierce the skin to deliver the vaccine. Its use speeded up the Smallpox Eradication Programme (see pages 16–17).

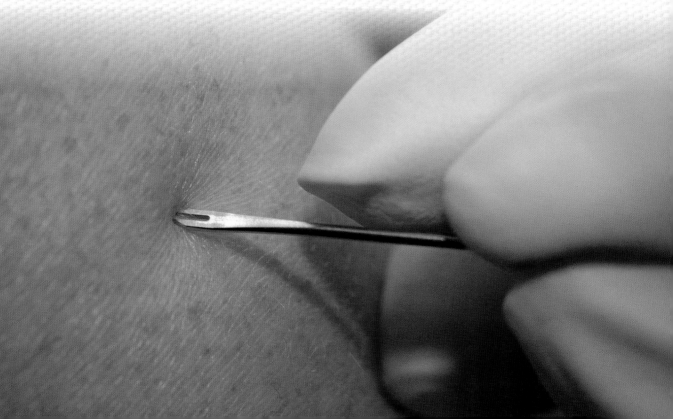

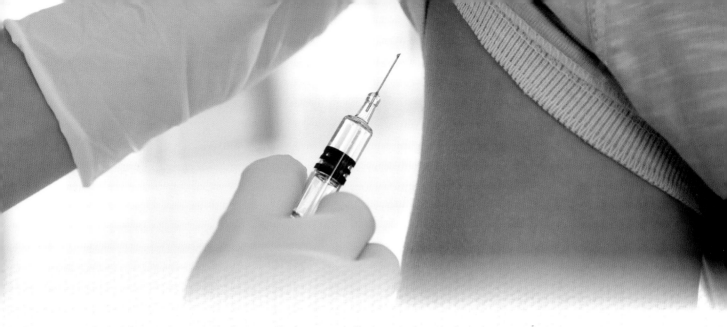

HOW FAST DO VACCINATIONS WORK?

It usually takes a week or two after a vaccination for your immune system to make enough antibodies to provide protection. Some vaccines give good protection after one dose, others require two or three doses to develop full immunity. Immunity is when your immune system remembers which antibody to use to fight a particular germ, protecting you from falling ill. Whilst some vaccines fade over time, others last a lifetime.

To be protected against flu, you have to have a vaccination each year. The vaccine used is changed slightly, to make it more likely to work against the ever-changing flu virus.

THE HERD

Although you probably think of a group of animals when you hear the word 'herd', scientists and doctors talk about herd immunity when they are referring to vaccination programmes. When about 80 per cent of a population has been vaccinated against a particular disease, the disease runs out of people to infect. This achieves herd immunity, protecting anyone who hasn't been vaccinated for whatever reason.

1. One person (shown in blue) catches an infectious disease. Most people have been vaccinated (shown in pink) against this disease.

2. The disease infects one other person but now it cannot spread any further as most people have immunity through vaccination.

Vaccinated person

Infected

Not vaccinated

HOW DO YOU VACCINATE THE WORLD?

Smallpox is the only infectious disease in people to have been wiped out by vaccination. It all started with Dr Jenner's vaccine in 1796 but it took until 1980 to eradicate the disease. The story of smallpox is also the story of how you vaccinate the world.

A NEW WORLD

After the end of the Second World War in 1945, governments worldwide were trying to build a new, better world. Part of this plan involved setting up the World Health Organization (WHO) in 1948 to improve the health of everyone. At a meeting in 1959, the Executive Board decided they must wipe out smallpox, a disease that continued to kill millions. The Smallpox Eradication Programme was going to be very expensive so a special budget was announced in 1966.

During the 20th century, children from wealthier countries were usually vaccinated against smallpox but elsewhere this was not happening. These children were vaccinated in Virginia, USA in 1946.

West Africa, 1968. Boys queue to be vaccinated by a healthcare worker using a jet injector gun. It was quick and easy to use but often broke down.

THE ERADICATION PLAN

In 1966 American doctor, Donald Henderson, was put in charge of the WHO programme. He realised that every country in the world needed to be involved by either supplying vaccines, equipment and money, or by providing healthcare workers in their countries to carry out the plan. He stressed the importance of tracking, tracing and isolating every case of smallpox and recording the information.

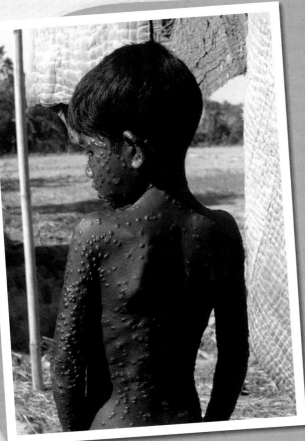

This child caught smallpox in Bangladesh in 1974.

The WHO team had a lot to organise. They needed posters and leaflets in many languages to advertise vaccination clinics and show people how to recognise the smallpox rash. Above all, they needed to train thousands of local people across Africa and Asia to vaccinate the population and track down cases.

RING VACCINATION

WHO staff taught local healthcare workers how to carry out ring vaccination. This involved showing people photos of people with the smallpox rash and asking to be led to anyone who had it. If it was smallpox, the healthcare worker quickly traced all the people who might have already caught smallpox and vaccinated them before they could develop the disease. This created a ring of immune people around each case of smallpox so the virus could not be passed on.

SUCCESS!

After a few years there were no cases in several African countries but, across India, the plan was not going so well. A breakthrough came in 1973, when WHO staff and the Indian government sent 120,000 people to visit every house in India over a ten-day period, identifying and then ring vaccinating a huge number of cases. Gradually smallpox was wiped out across the globe until there were no more cases anywhere in 1979. The following year the WHO announced that smallpox had been eradicated.

Ethiopia, India and Bangladesh were some of the last countries to be cleared of smallpox. In 1976 this Ethiopian child was vaccinated using a bifurcated needle.

WHO DISCOVERED OTHER IMPORTANT VACCINES?

Building on Dr Jenner's discovery of the first vaccine, others have developed vaccines against several infectious diseases. Read on for some brief accounts of vaccine breakthroughs since 1796.

Louis Pasteur made the rabies vaccine by experimenting on rabbits to produce a weak version of rabies, and then used it to create the vaccine.

LOUIS PASTEUR (1822-95)

No one knew how infectious diseases spread until French chemist and microbiologist, Louis Pasteur, proved that germs were the cause between 1860–64. From here, scientists began to identify exactly which germ caused each disease. Pasteur discovered how to make a vaccine against chicken cholera in 1879. He went on to develop a vaccine against anthrax in sheep and cattle in 1881. In 1884–85 he had another breakthrough when he discovered how to vaccinate animals and people against rabies.

EMIL VON BEHRING (1854–1917)

Diphtheria killed thousands of children every year. German bacteriologist Emil von Behring discovered how to treat diphtheria using a type of antibody, and this led to a vaccine used in vaccination programmes from the 1920s onwards. He also worked with Japanese physican Shibasaburo Kitasato (1852–1931) to develop a treatment for tetanus, used to save countless lives when it was first used during the First World War (1914–18). This also led to a tetanus vaccine.

Behring and Kitasato's tetanus serum used to treat tetanus in its original packaging, 1915.

DR JONAS SALK (1914-95) AND DR ALBERT SABIN (1906-93)

Polio (poliomyelitis) can kill or paralyse people. Long years of hard work by American doctor and medical researcher Jonas Salk gave the world the first polio vaccine in 1955. He once said: 'Hope lies in dreams, in imagination and in the courage of those who dare to make dreams into reality.' Another polio vaccine invented by Polish-American doctor and microbiologist Albert Sabin was ready in 1961. As it is given as drops into the mouth, this made it easy to use all over the world.

Two separate vaccines developed by Jonas Salk, shown right, and Albert Sabin have almost wiped out polio around the world.

DR PEARL KENDRICK (1890-1980) AND GRACE ELDERING (1900-88)

Sometimes it takes a long time to develop a really good vaccine against a disease. There had been vaccines against whooping cough since 1914 but they were not much good. It was the work of American research scientists, Dr Pearl Kendrick (left) and Grace Eldering, in the 1930s that created a vaccine that really worked in 1940.

Dr Pearl Kendrick worked with Grace Eldering at the Michigan Department of Health, USA.

DR MAX THEILER (1899-1972)

In the late 1920s, South African-American virologist Max Theiler and his team worked out that a virus causes yellow fever, a killer disease. Over the next ten years Theiler and his team tried out different ways of making a vaccine against the disease and were eventually successful. In 1938 people received the first yellow fever vaccinations.

DR LELAND CARMICHAEL (1930–2020) AND DR MAX APPEL (B. 1929)

It's not only people who are vaccinated – pets and farm animals are too. When canine parvovirus emerged in 1978, virologists Leland Carmichael and Max Appel at the Baker Institute for Animal Health at Cornell University, USA, developed a vaccine against the disease within three years. Later they built on their work to improve the vaccine.

The vaccine developed by Carmichael and Appel is still in use today and protects countless puppies from canine parvovirus, a virus that can kill puppies.

DR MAURICE HILLEMAN (1919-2005)

Over his lifetime, American microbiologist Maurice Hilleman created over 40 vaccines. These continue to save millions of children's lives every year. He led a team of research scientists at Merck and Company, a pharmaceutical company in the USA. He invented vaccines for MMR (mumps, measles and rubella), hepatitis A and B, meningitis, pneumonia and chicken pox.

Dr Maurice Hilleman developed the mumps vaccine in four years.

UN FOOD AND AGRICULTURE ORGANIZATION (FAO)

Other than smallpox (see pages 16–17), only rinderpest has been wiped off the planet by vaccination. Rinderpest is a deadly disease of cattle, buffalo and wild animals. Outbreaks of the disease have caused famines in the past. In 1945 the United Nation's Food and Agriculture Organization made the eradication of rinderpest one of its main aims. Different vaccines and tests started to help control the disease, but teamwork was the secret to success. Led by the FAO, vets, farmers, local people, governments and scientists worked together on an eradication campaign in the 1980s and 90s. In 2011 the world was declared free of rinderpest.

A Masai farmer looks after his cattle in Tanzania.

GAVI, THE VACCINE ALLIANCE

Gavi is an international organisation that brings together scientists, drug companies and funds to vaccinate children in the poorest countries. It also works to support the development of new vaccines, such as the vaccine against ebola. The support Gavi promised to vaccine manufacturers in 2014 speeded up trials (see pages 22–23) of an ebola vaccine, so that it could be used to save thousands of lives.

The ebola virus causes epidemics in West African countries. This deadly disease kills people as well as gorillas, monkeys and chimpanzees.

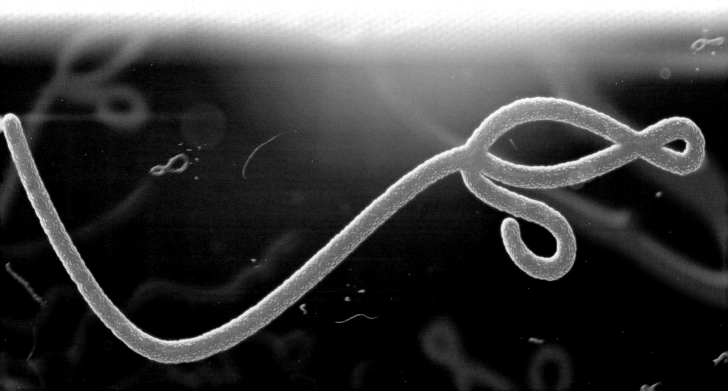

HOW DO PEOPLE CREATE A NEW VACCINE?

A new vaccine is the result of years of work by researchers, scientists, doctors and vaccine manufacturers. Let's look at how they do it.

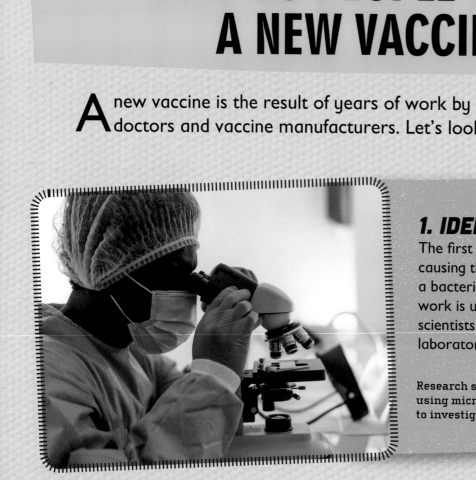

1. IDENTIFY THE GERM

The first step is to work out which germ is causing the infectious disease. Is it a virus, a bacterium, a fungus or a parasite? This work is usually carried out by research scientists at work in universities or small laboratories across the world.

Research scientists spend long hours using microscopes and other equipment to investigate diseases.

2. VACCINE RESEARCH

The next step is to work out how to make a vaccine against the germ. Can the germ be weakened or deactivated to make a vaccine? If this isn't possible, scientists look at the antigens (see page 5) on the outside of the germ. Can some of the antigens, or knowledge of the make-up of an antigen, be used to make a vaccine? Vaccine research can take years.

Whooping cough is caused by *Bordetella pertussis* bacteria, seen here (orange lozenges) through a microscope. Each bacterium has over 3,000 antigens but the vaccine only uses between three and five different antigens.

3. TEST, TEST, TEST

Each time scientists think they have created a vaccine they have to test it, first in the laboratory, then on animals and finally on a few people. At this point, a high number of vaccines fail to work, or are not safe enough to use. If a vaccine gets through this stage, vaccine manufacturers need to work out whether it is possible to make the vaccine in huge quantities.

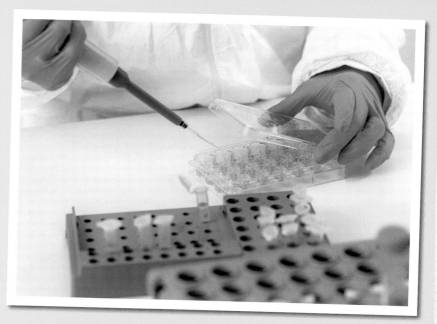

Research scientists repeat experiments to see if their idea works.

4. AND TEST SOME MORE

This is just the beginning of the tests that a vaccine needs to go through. Governments have their own vaccine and medicine regulators with strict rules requiring proof that a vaccine works and is safe. First the complete vaccine is tested on a few hundred people who are carefully watched for any side effects. If the vaccine gets through this step, the vaccine will be tested on several thousand people. All the tests are written up by scientists and studied in detail. It usually takes between eight and 15 years for a vaccine to be approved as safe to use.

Covid-19 vaccines (see pages 26–27) roll off the line in a Pfizer factory. Safety checks are carried out during the process of making vaccines in a factory.

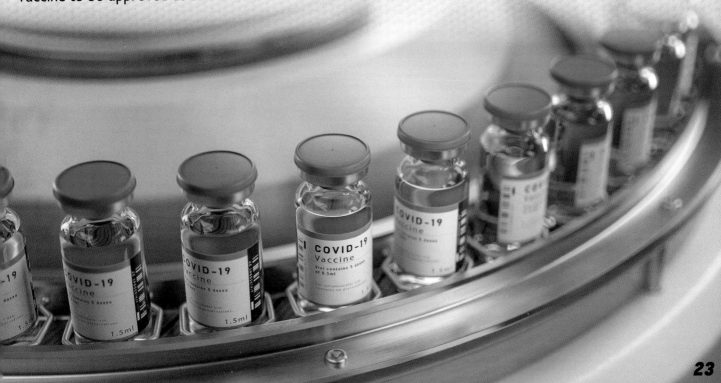

ANTI-VAXXERS AND VACCINE HESITANCY

Anti-vaccination groups and vaccine hesitancy appeared soon after Dr Jenner invented the smallpox vaccine in 1796. Some of the reasons for this remain the same – distrust of vaccine safety or of the people who want vaccinations to be taken up.

James Gillray's cartoon from 1802 shows Dr Jenner vaccinating a woman against smallpox. Gillray captures people's concerns about possible side effects from a vaccine that used material from cows.

UNDERSTANDING THE SCIENCE

It isn't all that surprising that some people distrusted the smallpox vaccine as even Dr Jenner himself didn't know how it worked. When people don't understand the science, it is easy for others to spread rumours, bad information or distrust. The same is true today.

FREEDOM TO CHOOSE

Governments around the world have at times used laws to force their citizens to vaccinate young children. This upset people in the past and continues to upset people who feel it should be their right to choose. Today many doctors and nurses feel people are more likely to accept vaccinations if they are given clear information about why they are a good idea and are allowed to ask questions, rather than being forced to accept them.

Using social media to spread the word, anti-vaxxers marched in cities around the world in 2020–21, protesting against Covid-19 vaccinations and wearing masks. This protest took place in New York, USA.

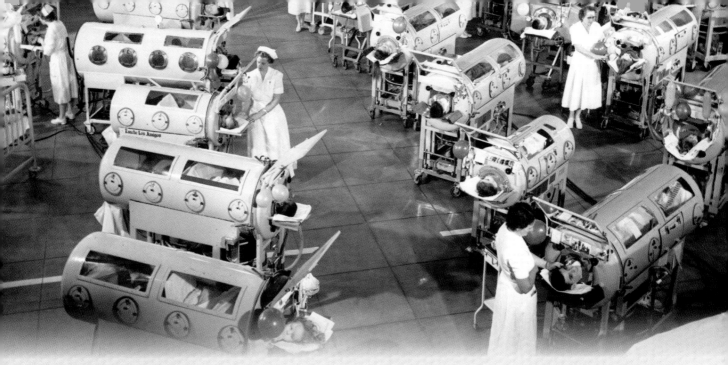

VACCINE SCARES

In 1955, a mistake at a vaccine factory in the USA created a batch of polio vaccines that gave children polio rather than protecting them from it. This event led to doubt about the safety of vaccines. It resulted in stricter safety rules for vaccine production.

Children being treated for polio after the Cutter vaccine disaster in April 1955. Sadly, ten children died and about 200 were left paralysed.

Sometimes a scare story can undo trust in vaccines for a large group of people. After British doctor, Andrew Wakefield (b. 1956), published a research paper linking the MMR vaccine with autism in 1998, parents across the world started to refuse the vaccine. Even though his research was proved wrong, Wakefield's 'bad science' continues to pass around the Internet.

When 52 people caught measles after visiting Disneyland, Florida, USA in December 2014, researchers discovered that low uptake of the MMR vaccination was the cause.

VACCINE HESITANCY

Vaccine hesitancy refers to people who are nervous or undecided about accepting vaccines for themselves, or their children. Sometimes very rare side effects from a vaccine can make someone lose trust in a vaccine or all vaccines. Other groups of people worry about vaccines because they don't trust their government or the drug companies who make vaccines, perhaps because they or their ancestors have been badly treated in the past.

COVID-19 VACCINES: A CASE STUDY

In December 2019, doctors in China noticed that their patients were dying of a disease they hadn't seen before. In January 2020, Chinese scientists released the genetic code of the virus that was causing the disease – severe acute respiratory syndrome coronavirus 2, or SARS-CoV-2 for short. As the disease spread around the world in 2020, killing millions of people, scientists started to search for a vaccine against the disease, named Covid-19.

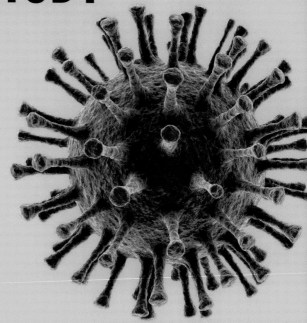

Like all coronaviruses, SARS-CoV-2 has spiky antigens on its surface. *Corona* means 'crown' in Latin.

In spring 2020, governments ordered people to stay at home to slow the spread of the disease. In Sydney, Australia, locked gates kept people from mixing together on beaches.

A RACE FOR A VACCINE

Around the world, almost 200 teams of scientists and doctors worked all hours to try to discover how to make a safe vaccine. Many put aside other important work and made research on a vaccine top of their to-do list. Their research was funded by national governments, drug companies, international organisations and individuals.

Teams of scientists took different approaches. Some used parts of the virus. Others used the genetic code of the virus and worked with that. Teams worked with different ways of making vaccines, old and new. They all built on research into other coronaviruses.

TESTING

Several of the teams shared their results with others to speed up the work, something that doesn't normally happen. Whenever scientists found something that might work, they tested it over and over again. Much of their work ended in failure.

mRNA VACCINES

Research into messenger ribonucleic acid vaccines (mRNA) has been going on for over 20 years. The scientists working for the Pfizer and Moderna drug companies decided to use this research to try to make a vaccine. mRNA vaccines teach our own cells to make the antigen spike on the surface of a virus, triggering our immune systems to make antibodies and T-cells that will protect us from that virus if we come across it in the future.

Scientists test their ideas about vaccines in laboratories.

VOLUNTEERS

Once some of the scientists had discovered safe vaccines that worked, they needed to run trials on volunteers – healthy people who wanted to play their part in finding a vaccine. A trial starts by giving a vaccine to a few people, then hundreds and finally thousands. Trials for multiple vaccines ran alongside other safety and testing checks, and preparations to make the vaccines in factories. This saved a lot of time but risked wasting a lot of money if a vaccine failed to work.

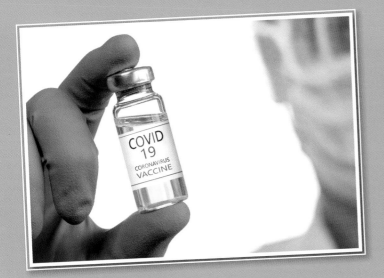

SUCCESS!

At the beginning of 2020, scientists could not promise they'd discover one vaccine against Covid-19 but, by the end of the year, two vaccines had been approved for emergency use in the UK, and in other countries afterwards. Further vaccines were approved, all developed in record time. The next challenge was to work out how to vaccinate the world, a huge task.

Covid-19 vaccine testing steps were run alongside each other, rather than one after the other, to save time. No steps were missed out.

WHAT'S THE FUTURE FOR VACCINATIONS?

So far, vaccinations have only eradicated smallpox in humans and rinderpest in cattle, but the WHO hopes that they'll soon succeed in wiping out polio as well. Scientists continue to search for vaccines against tropical diseases, different types of meningitis and flu, and against diseases that harm pets or farm animals. There will be more breakthroughs in the future.

REMEMBERING THE PAST

It's important to learn about the role vaccinations have played in improving the health of everyone. Growing up today, it's easy to forget how dangerous it was to catch smallpox or diphtheria, or for a pregnant woman to catch rubella. The rubella vaccine clearly shows that we don't just get vaccinated to protect ourselves, but to protect others. If you catch rubella, you should easily recover but if a pregnant woman catches it, her unborn baby could be harmed.

Dr Henderson (see page 16), second from left, is shown examining a smallpox vaccination scar on a little girl in Ethiopia, 1967. His plan helped eradicate smallpox completely.

RESPECTING NATURE

Researchers are working on vaccines against many diseases but, every now and then, a new disease becomes a problem. These diseases are usually caused by viruses in animals. Sometimes they change over time, making it possible for them to infect people. We need to prevent the need for new vaccines by respecting nature in different ways:

* leave wild animals alone
* leave their habitats intact
* stop hunting wild animals for meat
* and improve the way we care for farm animals.

Scientists think two recent pandemics were caused by viruses that passed from cave-dwelling bats to other animals and finally to humans.

NEW DEVELOPMENTS

New types of vaccine, including mRNA vaccines (see page 27), are much quicker to develop than older types of vaccine. They will help speed up the development of new vaccines and provide great hope for the future. Scientists are also working on better ways to get vaccines into the body, such as tiny vaccine patches. The patches are cheap and easy to store, unlike some vaccines that need to be stored in very cold fridges or they stop working.

WORKING TOGETHER

If governments, scientists, organisations and individuals work together they can fund vaccine research against diseases, share it, and make plans that will mean scientists and drug companies can spring into action if a new disease breaks out. Governments also need to work together to make sure vaccinations reach poorer countries as well as wealthy ones.

To protect everyone, vaccines need to be transported to the most remote parts of the world. These vaccines are arriving by bike for a vaccination session in Bangladesh.

GLOSSARY

acids In the stomach, these strong, liquid chemicals kill some germs.

anthrax A serious disease of sheep, cows and sometimes people.

anti-vaxxer A person who is against vaccinations.

antibody A substance (protein) produced by certain types of white blood cell to fight disease.

antigen A substance (often a protein) on the surface of cells, including germs, that usually triggers white blood cells to produce antibodies.

autism A brain condition that affects the development of communication skills.

bacterium/bacteria Tiny, single-celled living things. Some cause diseases.

bacteriologist A scientist who studies bacteria.

B-cell A type of white blood cell.

bifurcated needle A two-pronged needle used to introduce a vaccine under the skin.

canine parvovirus A serious disease that can lead to death in puppies due to diarrhoea.

cell One of the tiny building blocks that make up all living things.

chemist A scientist who studies chemistry.

chicken cholera A deadly disease of chickens.

chicken pox A disease that causes a fever and a rash.

coronaviruses A large family of viruses. Some of them cause diseases in humans or animals, and a few can pass from animals to humans.

Covid-19 A disease caused by a newly discovered coronavirus. It can cause many symptoms including a fever, cough, diarrhoea and pneumonia.

cowpox A mild disease of cows that can be caught by people.

deactivated To make something not work.

digest To break down something, such as food, so that it can be used by your body, for instance.

diphtheria A serious disease that makes it hard to breathe.

dose The right amount of a medicine or vaccine.

ebola A very serious disease that causes internal bleeding.

epidemic An outbreak of a disease over a large area of a country.

eradicate To wipe out or destroy something completely.

flu (influenza) An infectious disease causing a cold, a sore throat and a cough.

genetic code The instructions in a gene that tell the cell what to do.

germ A very small living thing, such as a virus, bacterium, parasite or fungus, that causes a disease.

Great Plague An epidemic of bubonic plague in England during 1665–66.

hepatitis A serious disease that affects the liver.

herd immunity When a population is protected from a particular disease because enough people are immune, usually achieved through vaccination.

hesitancy When someone is unsure about something, slowing down their desire to act.

immune You are immune when your immune system remembers which antibody or antibodies to use to fight a particular germ, protecting you from falling ill.

immune system The parts of your body that help protect it from invading germs.

immunisation The act of protecting someone from a disease, usually by vaccination (or variolation in the past).

infectious A disease that spreads easily between people.

injection Using a needle and syringe to inject a drug or vaccine into the body.

inoculation The act of protecting someone from a disease, usually by vaccination (or variolation in the past).

isolating Staying away from other people to prevent the spread of disease.

malaria A serious disease that causes fever and shivering, spread by some types of mosquito.

measles A disease that causes fever and a rash.

medical regulator The organisation in a country responsible for safety in all areas of healthcare.

meningitis A disease that causes the tissues covering the brain and spinal cord to swell.

microbe A tiny living thing such as a virus, bacterium, fungus or parasite.

microbiologist A scientist who studies all the tiny living things (microbes) which are too small to see without the use of a microscope.

microscope A scientific instrument used to make very small things larger. An electron microscope is a very powerful microscope.

mild A mild illness or disease is not serious.

mumps A disease that causes swellings of the face and neck.

pandemic An epidemic (a serious outbreak of a disease) occurring over a wide area, affecting several countries, or the whole world.

parasite A small animal or plant that lives on or inside another animal or plant.

pharmaceutical company A business, also known as a drug company, whose employees research, develop and bring to market medicines, including vaccines.

pneumonia A serious illness affecting one or both lungs.

polio A serious disease that can leave the infected person paralysed.

pus A liquid produced in a wound or spot as a result of an infection.

quarantine A period of time when someone has to stay away from others, to help prevent the spread of disease.

rabies A serious disease spread by a bite from an infected animal. It usually results in death.

rinderpest A serious disease of cows and other animals. It causes fever, diarrhoea and often death.

rotavirus A very bad stomach bug.

rubella (also known as German measles) A disease that causes a sore throat and a rash. It can damage unborn babies.

serum A clear liquid that can be separated from clotted blood.

side effect An extra, often unwanted, effect as a result of having a vaccination or taking a medicine to protect or cure you.

smallpox A deadly disease that caused a high fever and an awful rash.

T-cell A type of white blood cell.

tetanus A disease caused by bacteria entering the body through a cut or wound.

vaccination The act of introducing a vaccine into the body using an injection, nasal spray or other method.

vaccine A special medicine used to prevent a disease, or diseases.

vaccine manufacturer A business that makes vaccines in huge quantities.

variolation A way of protecting people against smallpox by introducing a tiny amount of smallpox material into the body.

virologist A scientist who studies viruses.

virus A very tiny living thing that can only reproduce inside other cells.

white blood cell A blood cell that helps to fight disease.

whooping cough A disease, often seen in children, that makes them cough and struggle to breathe.

yellow fever A deadly tropical disease.

WANT TO FIND OUT MORE?

Start with these websites:

https://vaccinemakers.org/lessons

https://www.immunology.org/celebrate-vaccines/public-engagement/activity-packs

INDEX

Franklin Watts
First published in Great Britain in 2021 by
The Watts Publishing Group

Copyright © The Watts Publishing Group, 2021

All rights reserved.

Editor: Sarah Peutrill
Designer: Lisa Peacock
Picture researcher: Diana Morris
Consultant: Alexandra R. A. Lee,
University College London

Franklin Watts
An imprint of
Hachette Children's Group
Part of The Watts Publishing Group
Carmelite House
50 Victoria Embankment
London EC4Y 0DZ

An Hachette UK Company
www.hachette.co.uk
www.hachettechildrens.co.uk

Printed in China

ISBN: 978 1 4451 8286 5 (HB)
ISBN: 978 1 4451 8288 9 (PB)
ISBN: 978 1 4451 8287 2 (Ebook)

The website addresses (URLs) included in this book were valid at the time of going to press. However, it is possible that contents or addresses may have changed since the publication of this book. No responsibility for any such changes can be accepted by either the author or the Publisher.

Every attempt has been made to clear copyright. Should there be any inadvertent omission please apply to the publisher for rectification.

Picture credits: Alamy: Agefotostock 27t; Alessandro Biascioli 22t; Nigel Baines: 5t, 13, 15b; Ian Dagnell 11b; Everett Collection 17t; Gado Images 14b, 16b; Granger Historical Picture Archive 28; Incamerastock 8; Marion Kaplan 17b; Paul Lovelace 26b; North Wind Picture Archives 18t; Pictorial Press 19t; Science History Images 10t; Science Photo Library 23t. Dreamstime: Wikto Wojtas 25b. Getty Images: Bettmann 25t; Science and Society Library 18b. Panos Pictures: G M B Akash 29b. Science Photo Library: Cecile Degremont/Look at Sciences 2b. Shutterstock: Ron Adar 24b; Airdone 4bl; all_about_people 20t; All-stock photos 29t; Aslysun back cover bl, 3b; Jim Barber 12; Christoph Burgstedt 5b; Everett Collection 9t; Fuadstephan 3t; Gorlov KV 2t; Gorodenkoff 23b; Jaddingt 21b; Kateryna Kon 22b; Midnight Movement back cover tr, 26t; New Africa 15t; Qari sb 4t; Pal Sand 27b; SciePro 4br; Aleksandar Todorovic 21. University of Michigan, Pearl L Kendrick Papers, PD 19b. U.S. NARA CC/PD 16t. Wellcome Library, London. Wellcome Images/ CCA CC BY 4.00 back cover tl, back cover br, 6t, 6b, 7b, 9b, 14t, 24t. Wikimedia commons/ CCA CC BY 4.00 7t, Jenner Museum /PD 11t, Walter Reed Medical Centre/PD 20b.